Christ The Rock Metro Church

Our Story

Christ The Rock Metro Church

Our Story

by

Valerie Bennett

ALPHA-OMEGA PUBLISHING
MEMPHIS, TN 38175

First printing 2002

Christ The Rock Metro Church - Our Story
ISBN 0-9719385-1-2

Alpha-Omega Publishing
P. O. Box 752424
Memphis, Tennessee 38175
(901) 368-6007

Dedication

This book is dedicated to my husband who is my best friend, my confidant, and my mentor, without whom there would be no Christ The Rock Metro Church Story.

To our children, Chris and Denise, who were so vital in pioneering this great work by helping us maintain our sense of humor. They were and are the joy of our lives and have made us very proud since they are now serving with us in this ministry.

To all the people who are and have been a part of Christ The Rock Metro Church. If it were not for you, we would not have this wonderful privilege of serving you. We love you. Thanks for believing in us.

Table of Contents

Acknowledgements

- To the Lord, Who by His grace and mercy counted us worthy of being part of His plan and purpose in establishing Christ The Rock Metro Church in Memphis Tennessee, and being able to share with you how He did it through us. He is a great God and this truly is His story. Thank you Holy Spirit for motivating me.

- To Reverend Everett Roseberry, Pastor of Greenland Devant United Methodist Church at that time, under whom we were born again, filled with the Holy Spirit, answered the call to ministry and then sent out, thank you. We appreciate your love, patience and the freedom to discover our giftings.

- To Cheryl Prewitt Salem, Miss America 1980, who by her testimony and joy of the Lord, opened our eyes to the Spirit-filled life at a Lay-Witness Mission. Thank you for the impartation.

- To Anne Giminez of Rock Church in Virginia Beach, Virginia, who through a prophecy confirmed in us the Word to go out and pioneer Christ The Rock Metro Church. Thank you for being a vessel of God.

- To my father-in-law, Fred M. Bennett, who showed me the love relationship between an earthly father and a daughter. It prepared me for the love relationship with my Heavenly Father. Thank you.

- To Denise, my daughter, who edited this story. Thank you. You could have been a marvelous English teacher, but God wanted you to impart life by teaching the youth.

- To Michelle Houston for encouraging me to complete this biography. Thank you for all your hard work, time, and expertise in assembling it. You are a blessing.

- To Stephanie Rooks for the cover design and Terri Mitchell for the back cover photo. Thanks, I really appreciate you both.

Preface

Dear Reader,

This book is a testimony of how Christ The Rock Metro Church came to be. I pray that as you read this story that God will speak to you and begin to cause a hunger in your heart to want to discover the call He has on your life so you can share that dream with others. This story has been in the making for nineteen years and only this year have I felt a release to finally tell it. Why? Because I know without a shadow of doubt that He did it all. There is no way I could have conjured up such a story. It is so biblical and needs to be told!

God uses imperfect people to do great things. We should not be envious or jealous but rejoice with them. We should shout it from the rooftops and boast about God's mighty feats. He is awesome! This is what I am doing. I want you to see and feel what He has done. Through this story, I want you to realize the potential He has placed inside each one of you. You are not merely here to please you, yourself, and yours. He has a plan and a purpose for your lives individually, as a family, as a church, and as a nation. You are all called to make a difference. There is no true life outside of God, and it is only in serving Him that you will feel a true sense of accomplishment, reward, and joy. Life is worth living.

As you read this testimony of how God used us and transformed us, my prayer for you is that you too will desire to embrace what He is doing in your life. He is ultimately writing His story through your testimony. Praise Him! You are being processed and perfected. Expect great things as you submit to His will and His Word.

Rejoicing in Him,

Valerie L. Bennett

Valerie L. Bennett

1
The Vision

Where there is no vision, the people perish;
Proverbs 29:18 KJV

Christ The Rock Metro Church was birthed August 1, 1983 in Collierville, Tennessee, just outside of Memphis. After having served five years in a United Methodist Church, my husband Fred and I felt the leading of the Holy Spirit to leave the denomination and pioneer a new work. God burned in our hearts a twofold vision. The first part of the vision was a desire to see the people of God set free to worship their Creator however they had the liberty to do so, whether raising hands, dancing, standing still, sitting, lying prostrate, kneeling, or clapping without feeling out of place. The Bible says in ***2 Corinthians 3:17, "Now the Lord is the Spirit; and where the Spirit of the Lord is, there is liberty."*** The second part of the vision was a church where people of any nationality, religious denominational background, and socioeconomic status could come together and worship God in spirit and in truth.

But the hour is coming, and now is, when the true worshipers will worship the Father in spirit and truth;... (John 4:23).

Leaving the United Methodist church came about after many prayers, much soul searching, lots of prophecies, and the gift of faith to step out and do it. We felt that we had accomplished all we were called to do in that particular church. It was time to move on with God. It had grown from thirty-five to three hundred people and it also became a Spirit-filled church. Leaving the denomination was similar to the children of Israel of the Old Testament, leaving Egypt and going on to the Promised Land. They moved when the cloud moved and stood still when it stopped moving. At night, it was a pillar of fire. That cloud represented God's protection and guidance.

And the Lord went before them by day in a pillar of cloud to lead the way, and by night in a pillar of fire to give them light, so as to go by day and night (Exodus 13:21).

We could not work within the framework of the denomination anymore because there were two visions. Division is another name for two visions. One was Methodist and we were more Inter-Denominational. The best thing for us to do was to part ways peacefully and amicably. We just wanted to follow the cloud that was moving for us. This principle was at work between Abraham and Lot in ***Genesis 13:8,9 (NIV) — Abram said to Lot,***

"Let's not have any quarreling between you and me, ...Let's part company."

Fred and I had both finished our education in May of 1983. Fred received his Master of Divinity from Memphis Theological Seminary and I received my Bachelor of Education from Memphis State University. We had diligently prepared ourselves for the next phase of our lives. We were spiritually and emotionally exhausted from all of our studies and from pastoring a church. Therefore, we went on a long overdue two-week family vacation in order to seek God for specific direction and to get rest that we desperately needed. We needed to get away in order to refocus on Jesus and see the next step He had for us. We knew we had to leave the denomination because we had served God and the people with all of our hearts and had finished the work He had assigned us to. We knew it was going to be different from anything we had ever known or seen in the Memphis area. We felt like Abraham, following God but not knowing where we were going.

Now the Lord had said to Abram: "Get out of your country, from your family and from your father's house, to a land that I will show you" (Genesis 12:1).

We took our children, Chris who at the time was nine and Denise who was six, on a vacation to Disney World in Florida and then we drove up the East Coast to Virginia Beach. We wanted to visit Rock Church, a church we had been watching on television. This church was different from any other church we had ever seen and experienced. In fact, we were deeply moved by what we saw: all kinds of people worshiping freely together however they felt comfortable. No one seemed to be intimidated by anyone or anything. The gifts of the Spirit flowed. It was so refreshing and real. It was life and not just religion.

As soon as we walked in the door, we ran into an old acquaintance who happened to be an elder of this church. We had no idea he attended this church. He invited Fred to meet the pastors. It so happened that they had him sit with the ministry team on the platform. Fred had the opportunity to see the whole congregation worship, firsthand. This was truly ordained of God in order to get him up front to get a better view of what he needed to see. A prophecy came forth by Pastor Anne Giminez, about why we were there. The gist of it was that we were there to see what we needed to see. We saw people of diverse backgrounds actually come together in the unity of the Spirit of God in the same room and worship together. Wow! We believed this was God impregnating us with the vision of Christ the Rock Metro Church. We decided then that this is what the Memphis area needed. For us it was a miracle in the making. It would truly have to be a "God thing." We knew that this was it! We could finally verbalize what we felt in our hearts and what we had seen in the Spirit realm. God used that church to show us what was needed in this great city of Memphis. We will be forever grateful. Praise God!

We had always been told that in order to build a great church it had to be homogeneous, otherwise it would not work. Our hearts could not concur with that idea so we rejected it silently not being able to prove or disprove that fallacy. It is a lie that the enemy has used over and over again in this city to keep everyone divided along racial and denominational lines. Jesus quotes in the Gospel of ***John 8:44 — "You are of your father the devil, and the desires of your father you want to do. He was a murderer from the beginning, and does not stand in the truth, because there is no truth in him. When he speaks a lie, he speaks from his own resources, for he is a liar and the father of it"*** (lies). Indeed the most segregated time in our city is during the Sunday morning church hour. Were we going to believe the father of lies or the Father of Creation?

After receiving the impartation of this vision, we knew specifically what our calling was and what God wanted for this city. We were to go home and do it no matter what the cost. We were pregnant with that seed to see a church where racial discrimination no longer existed and where people could come together in the love of Jesus regardless of former church affiliation or socioeconomic stance. We knew what our calling was for the city of Memphis and our hearts have burned with that vision ever since. We live to see the reality of that vision come to pass. We knew God spoke to our hearts and what He says always comes to pass. He is ready (or watching) to perform His Word (Jeremiah 1:12). That means He is making sure it will happen.

"So is my word that goes out from my mouth: It will not return to me empty, but will accomplish what I desire and achieve the purpose for which I sent it" (Isaiah 55:11 NIV).

Just as we were returning to Memphis, Fred was offered a wonderful job to work in a ministry in Virginia Beach. We had watched a particular TV Christian program and Fred said, "How awesome it would be to work for that ministry." The opportunity presented itself while we were in Virginia Beach, right after we received the call to pioneer a different kind of church in Memphis. Thus the test came. We had just accepted in our hearts the vision to pioneer a church in Memphis and then this door of opportunity was opened to us. What a challenge! What a temptation! Fred had a wrestling match. Was he going to follow God's desire or the desire of his heart? Both were very good choices, but to obey and serve God are better because it means reaping the hundredfold blessings. We had no choice but to do what God put in our hearts. He had given us a vision and a purpose—a picture of all kinds of people worshiping together in unity. This was to be our call and we could not get away from it. We had been seeing and feeling something in our spirits that would be different from the status quo. We could not explain this to anyone because we could not put it into words. The reason was it did not exist in this city as far as we knew. The vision we were to pioneer was to be:

A church filled with the Spirit and all kinds of people,
fulfilling the great commission,
reconciling us to God and one another.

This is our church motto and it is our vision and purpose. In other words, we would build a city church, a great army on the cutting edge that would pull down the walls of

gender and racial division, denominationalism, and any other type of division in the city of Memphis and surrounding areas bringing about reconciliation. ***2 Corinthians 5:18*** says, ***"Now all things are of God, who has reconciled us to Himself through Jesus Christ, and given us the ministry of reconciliation."*** We were to be a prototype of the Kingdom of God! God wants His Church to be in unity. Jesus wants us to be one. He spoke of this in ***John 17:21 — "that they all may be one, as You, Father, are in Me, and I in You; that they also may be one in Us, that the world may believe..."***
The Apostle Paul also taught us this same lesson about unity in ***Galatians 3:28 — "There is neither Jew nor Greek, there is neither slave nor free, there is neither male nor female; for you are all one in Christ Jesus."***
We will all be together one day in heaven, therefore we need to learn now how to live together on this earth as one people. This is God's will in the earth.

Even when we were dead in trespasses, made us alive together with Christ (by grace you have been saved), and raised us up together,...(Ephesians 2:5,6)

The only way we can be in unity is by practicing righteousness and walking in love. We can do this because we have the Lover living inside of us.

Beloved, if God so loved us, we also ought to love one another (1 John 4:11), ...for God is love (1 John 4:8).

This is the very nature of God, and we must allow His Spirit to take preeminence in our lives. In other words, we must allow the Word of God to have ascendancy in our everyday lives. Memphis needs a good dose of righteousness because it is so torn, so divided especially along racial lines, being the city where Martin Luther King Jr. was assassinated. The government does enact many laws, but it does not matter because an agency cannot bring about unity or a change of heart. Only the Holy Spirit can do this. ***For it is God who works in you to will and to act according to His good purpose (Philippians 2:13 NIV).*** It is an inside job! Old mindsets, biases, and prejudices have to be eradicated from our very being. We need a new way of thinking, which only comes through God giving us a new heart.

"I will give you a new heart and put a new spirit within you; I will take the heart of stone out of your flesh and give you a heart of flesh. I will put My Spirit within you and cause you to walk in My statutes, and you will keep My judgments and do them. Then you shall dwell in the land that I gave to your fathers; you shall be My people, and I will be your God. I will deliver you from all your uncleanness..." (Ezekiel 36:26-29).

We believe God is going to accomplish this. He always does what He says. We also believe we have been called for such a time as this. We are *like* ***Esther 4:14 - "For if you remain completely silent at this time, relief and deliverance will arise for the Jews*** (we could substitute Memphians) ***from another place, but you and your father's house will perish. Yet who knows whether you have come to the kingdom for such a time as this?"*** We cannot do it alone, but God can through a multitude of His people. He is looking for a mighty army that will pull down strongholds and set the captives free. This is the vision of Christ The Rock Church. It must be kept before the people at all times. The Bible tells us in ***Habakkuk 2:2-3 — "...Write the vision and make it plain on tablets, That he may run who reads it. For the vision is yet for an appointed time; But at the end it will speak, and it will not lie. Though it tarries, wait for it; Because it will surely come, It will not tarry."***

Following God is not always the easy way, and it means suffering persecution from family and friends. It does not matter because it is worth it. Serving God is the most rewarding experience. It means letting God have full rein of your life. It also means giving up personal desires for the Kingdom of God. Jesus says in ***Matthew 16:24 — "...If anyone desires to come after Me, let him deny himself, and take up his cross, and follow Me."*** It means putting God first no matter what. It means trusting Him completely to do what He said He would, since He is not a liar.

We have had to plow where no one has plowed before. It means going against the flow of what everyone is doing. It means rejecting what has been the standard for decades and decades. It also means rejecting the status quo. We could not accept the saying: "This is just the way it is, so accept it." We did not see the full picture ourselves until we embarked on this journey. God has been unveiling it step by step and it is ongoing even now as you read this story. He has kept us on His course. He does it by His Word. He truly does love us to be that diligent.

Your word is a lamp to my feet and a light to my path (Psalm 119:105). He truly does order our steps.

The steps of a good man are ordered by the Lord, And He delights in his way (Psalm 37:23).

When we left the denomination, the thought of failure never crossed our minds. It was not part of our vocabulary either.

Death and life are in the power of the tongue, And those who love it will eat its fruit (Proverbs 18:21).

I believe we were given *"the gift of faith,"* one of the gifts of the Spirit as listed in 1 Corinthians 12. The Bible tells us in ***Philippians 4:13 — I can do all things through Christ who strengthens me.*** We were and are compelled to go on with God wherever He leads regardless of the cost (2 Corinthians 5:14). In other words, His love motivates us. We choose to please God rather than man. It does not matter what people think or say about us. We have always felt God's hand on us, a hand of direction, a hand of strength, and a hand of protection. This is why we are able to trust Him. ***Proverbs 3:5-6*** says, ***"Trust in the Lord with all your heart, and lean not on your own understanding; In all your ways acknowledge Him, and He shall direct your paths."***

Serving God and fulfilling the call of God on our lives (the vision and purpose of "Christ The Rock Metro Church") is what keeps us going. Our hearts burned with this vision because it was ordained by God. He chose us in Him before the foundation of the world...(Ephesians 1:4). He chose us and prepared us beforehand to pioneer this great work that would have an influence far and wide. It is such an honor and a privilege to serve Him and the people of this great city. We are awed and humbled at what God is doing here. We know without a shadow of a doubt that we have been called to the city of Memphis, and out of this church a ministry to its surrounding areas and even the nations.

God brought us to Memphis even before we knew Him. He had plans to save us and put His Spirit inside of us and use us to pioneer Christ The Rock Metro Church. What a privilege! I am so glad we did not miss our destiny! He empowered us.

"But you shall receive power when the Holy Spirit has come upon you; and you shall be witnesses to Me in Jerusalem, and in all Judea and Samaria, and to the end of the earth" (Acts 1:8).

We are seeing the walls of division come down slowly but surely. God is faithful. He wants His people to be in unity. Jesus says in ***John 17:22 — "And the glory which You gave Me I have given them, that they may be one just as We are one."*** There are only two kinds of people on this earth, two races: the believers and the nonbelievers, the ones who receive Jesus in their hearts and those who reject Him. When we receive Him in our hearts, we become part of God's family. We are a chosen generation, a royal priesthood, a holy nation, His own special people (1 Peter 2:9). It really does not matter what walk of life people come from because after God gets hold of them, He changes them and they become like Him.

Therefore, if anyone is in Christ, he is a new creation; old things have passed away; behold, all things have become new (2 Corinthians 5:17).

He bought and paid for them with the precious blood of His Son, Jesus.

For God so loved the world that He gave His only begotten Son, that whoever believes in Him should not perish but have everlasting life (John 3:16).

We are all equal in God's eyes because we begin the race at the same place and we all win, provided we finish our course. The differences that we encounter are in function only. The Bible says in ***Genesis 1:27 — "So God created man in His own image; in the image of God He created him; male and female He created them."*** Therefore, we all have worth in Him.

2

Our Testimonies

And they overcame him by the blood of the Lamb and by the word of their testimony, and they did not love their lives to the death.
Revelation 12:11

Every Christian has a story to tell of how they came to know the reality of Jesus and how they came to live and serve Him. I believe I must give you a brief history of our lives that led us to pioneer this great work. It really is His Story enacted through us. It is always exciting to see how He orders our steps and directs our paths. Looking back on our lives, He has always had His hand on us even when we were not aware of His presence. In fact, He is drawing all men to Himself but not all will answer the call. His desire is for all men to be saved and to come to a knowledge of the truth (1 Timothy 2:4).

Peter quoted the Prophet Joel in ***Acts 2:17 — "And it shall come to pass in the last days, says God, That I will pour out My Spirit on all flesh; your sons and your daughters shall prophesy, Your young men shall see visions, Your old men shall dream dreams."*** He promised us that He would not leave us alone, but to be with us even to the end of the age (Matthew 28:20). He would send the Holy Spirit to help us. Jesus said in ***Luke 24:49 — "Behold, I send the Promise of My Father upon you..."*** In fact, this is when the universal Church was birthed, on the day of Pentecost, 2000 years ago. Jesus is in the world wooing and drawing people to Himself.

Let me tell you what God has done in our lives to bring us to where He has us now, Pastors of Christ The Rock Metro Church. He has done a marvelous job of drawing us and changing us. It has been an awesome journey following Him. The Bible tells us to declare His deeds among the peoples, for He has done excellent things (Isaiah 12:4-5), and this is what I want to do. We have a testimony of what God has done in our lives and we want to share it. I believe it will minister to you. What He has done for us, He will do for you, since He is no respecter of persons.

I will praise You, O Lord, with my whole heart; I will tell of all Your marvelous works (Psalm 9:1).

Valerie

I was born March 25, 1947, in the city of Edmundston, the province of New Brunswick, Canada which borders on the French province of Quebec and the State of Maine, USA. Needless to say, it is culturally very French and very Roman Catholic. I am the eldest of eight children. I have five sisters and two brothers, and we were all born in the span of ten years. My mother was British born and reared, and my father was French Canadian. They married during World War II. After the war, she immigrated to Canada. We grew up being bilingual. I do not remember ever not being able to speak French. I started out the first two grades in English then transferred to a French neighborhood school. From that point on, we received all our instruction at school in French and spoke it everywhere except in our home. At home, we communicated in English because of my mother. As kids, when we communicated, we switched back and forth between French and English without even realizing it (much to the aggravation of my mother). She always thought it very rude to speak French amongst ourselves, when she was present.

My mother was a converted Catholic, so we did not do a lot of the rituals many of the people did in their homes, such as recite the rosary as a family. We did, however, go to church. Either my Mum or Dad took us when we were little. We never went as a family, since there were too many babies. We received most of our Catholic training at school. The government used the Convent to house public education for girls from junior high through senior high school. Most of my teachers were nuns. The boys had their own junior and high schools and were taught by Catholic brothers. Needless to say, coeducation was a foreign concept.

My early childhood was a happy one. My siblings probably do not remember this because my father's alcoholism was quite advanced by the time they were old enough to remember anything about him. By the time I was in the seventh grade, our home life left much to be desired. My father's alcohol abuse had become uncontrollable. I remember being very depressed over the whole situation. I felt such shame, rejection, humiliation and embarrassment. I had an inferiority complex and very low self-esteem. I felt everyone looked down on me because of the situation at home. I did not know that my friends and classmates had their own struggles with which to contend. There was never enough money to provide for the necessities of life such as food and clothes. There was definitely no peace except when Dad was absent. It was stressful wondering where he was when he was not working. I remember being very angry with God for not answering the one prayer I prayed over and over again. It was to change the situation at home. I was begging God because I did not know how to pray in faith. I wished God would stop my dad from drinking so that we could all be a happy family again. I felt the pain and disappointment in Mum.

The answer did not come, so I reasoned that there was no God. I literally recall turning my head in my bedroom and saying out loud: "I shall not believe You anymore because You do not exist. If You did, You would have changed the situation." And that was that! However I still continued to practice the religious rituals because that was the culturally correct thing to do, since I was a Roman Catholic. I had participated in all the necessary requirements of the faith. I remember my First Communion, my Confirmation, my Solemn Communion, the monthly confessions with the priest, praying the rosary every night, mass on Sundays, and many other rites. Being religious was a way of life, a front. It was part of the cultural persona. I had some sort of respect for God. He was this Supreme Being. I had no personal relationship with Him. I felt no love for Him and I felt none from Him, only a fear of going to hell. This, along with peer pressure to fit in, motivated me to continue attending mass and to perform all the ritual practices. Once in college, I stopped attending mass. I had finally severed myself from this ritualistic way of life. I was going to do what I wanted to do and not please people anymore. I did not have a personal relationship with the Lord because I was not yet born again. These rituals were a form of dead religion. It had no life, and I had had enough. Jesus said in the Gospel of ***John 3:3 — "Most assuredly, I say to you, unless one is born again, he cannot see the kingdom of God."*** I do not ever remember anyone ever asking me if I was born again or being told that I needed to be saved in order to become a Christian. I was taught that being born into a Catholic family automatically guaranteed Heaven after death. What a lie! ***John 14:6*** says, ***"I am the way, the truth, and the life. No one comes to the Father except through Me."*** Another important Scripture is found in ***Ephesians 2:8*** which says, ***"For by grace you have been saved through faith, and that not of yourselves; it is the gift of God."*** Because of my unhealthy fear of God, I had no concept of His love for me. I thought of Him as an angry strict disciplinarian ready to zap me, if I did anything wrong.

As a child growing up, I played school and I taught everything that moved and didn't move. I was always the teacher. I was going to be a schoolteacher, and I was going to be a good one. I was highly motivated to become somebody. I was not going to be a loser in this life. So needless to say, I grew up knowing that I would be a teacher. That was my desired career for life.

I graduated with honors from high school because I used education and books as an escape from reality. I then went on to Teachers College. This two-year program enabled me to fulfill that lifelong desire. The government had established a special program, which allowed students to attend tuition free as long as they promised to teach in the province of New Brunswick for six years. Not being very prosperous, this definitely was the way to go for me. I would be licensed to teach and finish my bachelor's degree in the evenings and summers. It was a great program. It was God's hand and I had not recognized it. Issues at home clouded my visibility. I felt God had let me down, or so I perceived. I thought that if I was going to succeed in this life and get into a teaching career, I was going to have to do it all myself. I worked hard in the summer to supplement what the government did not provide because I did not want to burden my family. My mentality was that I was going to be in control of my life and succeed without the help of anyone. I was tired of always needing or lacking. I would provide for myself, since I could not trust anyone on this earth or in Heaven. This was the mindset I had acquired because of my life experience. It was one of independence and self-centeredness because I was bound and determined to succeed. I had to succeed because I wanted a better quality of life for myself than what I had experienced thus far. I could not depend on anyone and I certainly could not trust God, since I felt He had let me down. I did not know what the Gospel promised in ***John 10:10 — "The thief does not come except to steal, and to kill, and to destroy. I have come that they may have life, and that they may have it more abundantly."*** I was experiencing the first part of that Scripture only. I did not know the Lord.

As soon as I graduated from college, I was hired to teach junior high in a little school near where my French Canadian grandmother lived. She was special and I loved her very much. I called her "Memere." She would tell me as a little girl that I would teach in the school behind her house and have lunch with her every day. It happened just the way she said it would. This was the fulfillment of a dream my grandmother and I shared. I believed it was prophetic. She probably would not call it that, but that is what it really was. I believed her and hung onto her words and that dream. She was God-fearing because she went to mass every morning and prayed for her family. I believe she prayed for me to have that position. The Bible tells us in ***Psalm 37:4 — "Delight yourself also in the Lord, And He shall give you the desires of your heart."*** I did not know God personally, but my grandmother did. My desire was granted because of her prayers for me. In fact, my parents would always introduce me to people as the future schoolteacher. Words carry weight and they are prophetic and self-fulfilling. We have to be careful of the words we speak over ourselves. We must speak words of life, words that edify and build, rather than tear down. Words create a particular atmosphere or ambiance.

Death and life are in the power of the tongue, and those who love it will eat its fruit (Proverbs 18:21).

It is also important to watch what we allow to fill us because sooner or later it will come out of us. "*...**For out of the abundance of the heart the mouth speaks. For by your words you will be justified, and by your words you will be condemned" (Matthew 12:34,37).*** I felt proud to be introduced as a future teacher. I never deviated from that vision. I never wondered about what I was going to be when I grew up. I always felt encouraged to go on even when life was difficult.

I did not have a personal relationship with God but He was watching over me and was preparing me for my husband and our life's work. Three months into my new career, I met Fred L. Bennett, a United States Airman, and thus our life together begins. Destiny has started.

But as it is written: "Eye has not seen, nor ear heard, Nor have entered into the heart of man the things which God has prepared for those who love Him" (1 Corinthians 2:9).

Fred

Fred, the eldest of four children, three boys and one girl, was reared in Memphis, Tennessee, by God fearing parents. He had godly grandmothers who were also role models of godliness in his life. He attended church and Sunday school every Sunday of his life from the time he was a little boy until he went into the military. He was very involved in "MYF," the Methodist Youth Fellowship. His parents were very involved in all aspects, especially the choir. His mother played the piano and his dad sang tenor and often led the choir. In fact, Fred said that he thought his family had been assigned to turn the lights on and off because they were there every time the doors were open and the last to leave. Their whole lives revolved around the church. They were people who truly loved and served God and His church with all diligence. He had a rich heritage even though he says he did not have a personal relationship with the Lord at that time. He was not yet born again. Jesus said in the Gospel of ***John 3:3— "...Most assuredly, I say to you, unless one is born again, he cannot see the kingdom of God."***

Fred attended all white local public schools because of segregation. Desegregation laws had not been enacted until the early seventies. He says he "escaped from school." He barely graduated from high school. It was not because he lacked intelligence but because he was not motivated. He says he did not know who he was and what his calling in life was. He needed direction. The reason he made it through school was that he was and still is an avid reader and has a great memory. He is the one person you want on your team if you are playing the game of "Trivia Pursuit". He has a wealth of knowledge! He has always been an excellent communicator who knows how to interact with people. He is very polite, due to his southern gentility upbringing. He is well versed in current events and politics and could debate you on any issue. If he were not in the ministry today, he probably would have been a great politician.

God had been preparing him way back then because he was revolted by the hypocrisy he saw in the area of racial discrimination and prejudice that was so prevalent as he was growing up.

There is neither Jew nor Greek, there is neither slave nor free, there is neither male nor female; (black or white) ***for you are all one in Christ Jesus (Galatians 3:28).***

This Biblical principle needed to be taught and practiced. He was very disturbed by the racial inequality of African Americans that he had seen growing up. He wanted to do something about this division. He wanted the hearts of the people to be open towards one another. He felt righteous indignation because he knew the constitution said that all men were created equal and that they had undeniable rights. He had a heart for reconciliation even in the early sixties.

2 Corinthians 5:18 Now all things are of God, who has reconciled us to Himself through Jesus Christ, and has given us the ministry of reconciliation (2 Corinthians 5:18).

God was preparing him for Christ The Rock Metro Church. In fact, on one of our dates he told me that when he was a little boy he had once contemplated becoming a minister. That really impressed me. He says he does not remember telling me this. His father once told me that he had prayed for his eldest son to be in the ministry.

After high school, he went to a local university for about a year before enlisting in the US Air Force, instead of being drafted by the US Army. His grandmother gave him a Bible and highlighted a Scripture in the Gospel of ***John 6:63 — It is the Spirit who gives life; the flesh profits nothing. The words that I speak to you are spirit, and they are life.*** This was during the Vietnam War. He chose this route instead of being sent to the paddy fields of Vietnam. He attended basic training in Texas and tech school in Illinois before being sent to his first tour of duty at Loring Air Force Base in the state of Maine. He was part of SAC, Strategic Air Command, and he worked as an electrician on B-52's. It was then that our saga of life together began.

"...He has put eternity in their heart"
(Ecclesiastes 3:11).

3

Oneness

Two are better than one, Because they have a good reward for their labor.
Ecclesiastes 4:9

As soon as I began teaching, I met Fred in the small town of Madawaska in northern Maine, not long after he arrived there. We were still not born again at that time. We were natural beings. ***The natural man does not receive the things of the Spirit of God, for they are foolishness to him; nor can he know them, because they are spiritually discerned (1 Corinthians 2:14).*** He was different from anyone else I had ever met. I did not know how to explain what I saw in him, besides the obvious, his good looks and fun loving personality. But now, I know that it was divine purpose and destiny. I felt deep down he was going somewhere in life and I wanted to go where he was going. I could not settle for a run-of-the-mill or an ordinary sort of guy. ***Jeremiah 29:11 says, "For I know the thoughts*** (plans) ***that I think toward you, says the Lord, thoughts*** (plans) ***of peace*** (welfare) ***and not of evil, to give you a future and a hope."*** After one date, I felt I could spend the rest of my life with him. This seemed very strange to me because I had never had such an experience. I was not in love yet because I did not know this man. Fred said that one look at me settled it for him.

He who finds a wife finds a good thing, And obtains favor from the Lord (Proverbs 18:22).

I believe God puts people together to fulfill His plan and purposes in this earth, in order to bring about His Kingdom. He does, however, give us the option of choosing. Fred and I are testimonies of the plan of our Lord. It is almost like we were pawns used of God in a righteous way to fulfill His plan He had for Memphis and the surrounding area.

After a short courtship of almost eight months, we were married in Saint-Basile Catholic Church, July 23, 1968. It was the church I had attended as a kid. I thought our wedding was cool! I was a Catholic, my husband-to-be was a Protestant, and the best man was Jewish. What an example or foreshadow of what was to come. We were not aware of this prophetic picture we would later see fulfilled in our ministry. Three days later, Fred left for Guam, courtesy of the United States Air Force, to do a four-month tour of duty without me. He returned home to his base in Maine for eight months and was sent to Thailand for another tour of duty. This time it was for one year. What a way to begin a marriage! We would begin to get adjusted to being together and then he would be sent away again. I was teaching at the time, so this kept me sane and busy.

Living during the Vietnam conflict made it very difficult for a couple to stay together because of so many separations due to military assignments. However, we did have a strong love and determination to make it work, though we spent most of our first two years apart. We believed our marriage vows were forever. We were both reared with the idea that marriage is forever, for better or for worse, in sickness and in health, till death do us part. We still did not know the Lord but looking back He had His hand on us, protecting and preserving us for His plan and purpose to unfold in our lives. Upon returning from Thailand, we were sent to Massachusetts for the duration of Fred's military service.

Upon Fred's discharge from the military in January of 1971, we moved to Memphis. Our plans to return to Canada had been overruled by the Lord. Our steps were ordered by Him (Psalm 37:23). Fred did not want to return to Memphis, but it was the only door open to us. God knew what was going to happen, and He was ordering our steps to get us to a place where we would answer the call He had for our lives.

"Before I formed you in the womb I knew you; Before you were born I sanctified you; I ordained you a prophet to the nations" (Jeremiah 1:5).

Memphis was very different for me. The weather was unbearable because I was not accustomed to such heat and humidity. I was accustomed to four seasons and this part of the country only has two. I was in culture shock. I did not know what language to speak. I was accustomed to French or English. I could not speak southern nor did I understand it. The people were very different to me and there was the racial factor, a new experience for me. I had never been in this kind of environment. I watched and listened. There were many things I did not understand or like. I was also very homesick for my family and my country. I was not adjusting well at all. We were not experiencing abundant living because we did not have the Abundant Life Giver: Jesus living in our hearts.

In 1973, our fifth year of marriage, we began to have problems because we had no solid foundation. We were both too independent in some ways probably due to our long separations during our military days. We were dependent on each other in other ways because I expected Fred to meet my every need, and he looked to me to meet his every need. We were unable to do this. Therefore, we became disappointed, frustrated, and angry at each other.

Needless to say, the honeymoon period was definitely over. We had begun our wilderness time in our marriage. It was a time of testing. During those times, the end result would be either victory or defeat. It looked like the latter was going to happen. We had placed our faith in each other rather than in God. We had become co-dependent on each other. Only God can meet our needs and desires. Our marriage began to crumble and we did not know how to save it. Jesus said in The Gospel of ***Matthew 7:24-27***:

"Therefore whoever hears these sayings of Mine, and does them, I will liken him to a wise man who built his house on the rock: and the rain descended, the floods came, the winds blew and beat on that house; and it

did not fall, for it was founded on the rock. But everyone who hears these sayings of Mine, and does not do them, will be like a foolish man who built his house on the sand: and the rain descended, the floods came, and the winds blew and beat on that house; and it fell. And great was its fall."

We loved each other but we did not know how to live with each other. We made each other miserable. We had not made Jesus the Savior and Lord of our lives. Without Him, marriages do not last and if they do, there is no joy or happiness in them, just merely a co-existence. A husband and a wife need Jesus. The following Scripture talks about a cord of three strands being strong. I believe the three strands are Jesus, the husband and the wife.

Two are better than one, Because they have a good reward for their labor. For if they fall, one will lift up his companion. But woe to him who is alone when he falls, For he has no one to help him up. Again, if two lie down together, they will keep warm; But how can one be warm alone? Though one may be overpowered by another, two can withstand him. And a threefold cord is not quickly broken (Ecclesiastes 4:9-12).

God promised us abundant life in His Word, the Bible. "... ***I have come that they may have life, and that they may have it more abundantly" (John 10:10b)***. But we were far from experiencing it. In fact, we were experiencing the first part of that Scripture — ***The thief does not*** come ***except to steal, and to kill, and to***

destroy (John 10:10a). We were not communicating anymore. It got to the point where we had built walls between us. So, I flew back home to Canada. I thought our marriage was over. I hated the word divorce, but I thought I had no alternative but to divorce him and go on with my life.

During this time I had begun to look to God, something I had not done since the seventh grade. I clipped the serenity prayer out of the newspaper and read it several times a day. It was so strange, but it would give me comfort. I was leaning on God. I believe He gave me the strength to keep on going. He was the only anchor that gave me hope and comfort at that time (Hebrews 6:19).

Little did I know that my in-laws were praying for us. As soon as I arrived home, I received a letter from one of Fred's grandmothers. She told me she loved me and was praying for me. I had never had anybody say that to me, and it broke my heart. I just wept. It softened me so that when Fred called and asked if I would consider returning, I said that I would if he agreed to three conditions. First, we needed to go to church. Secondly, I wanted to start a family. Thirdly, he had to change to a day job. To my surprise he agreed. I saw how his parents loved each other and treated one another with respect, and I wanted that for us. They were a model couple for me, and the one variable I saw was that they regularly attended church. There must be something to this church attendance, and I wanted to experience this for myself. They also had nice friends they ate out with every Sunday after church. They all seemed to love each other and care for one another. We needed new friends and we also needed a social life. We were hungry for godly relationships.

We began attending the Methodist Church with Fred's family. It seemed very plain in comparison to what I had been accustomed: a Catholic Church with many statues (icons) and rituals. It was refreshing. There were a few similarities, such as Bible readings and prayer recitation. They stood like I was accustomed to, but they did not kneel, genuflect, or do the sign of the cross. I liked it, because it was different. I was impressed with Fred because he knew exactly what to do and when to do whatever was required. It was as though he had never left church, although he had not been in one the past eight years. It felt good to me to be in church. I felt safe and loved. In fact, it provided stability and fellowship that we so desperately needed. I loved church and I could say with the Psalmist in ***Psalm 122:1 —I was glad when they said to me, "Let us go into the house of the Lord."***

I wondered how long Fred would go along with this, but to my relief he did. He was a man of his word, a man of integrity and character. God was healing us. We were beginning to trust one another again. God is a good God. Praise Him! I give Him all the glory and praise for saving our marriage. Our love for each other increased because we were being yoked to Jesus.

"Take My yoke upon you and learn from Me, for I am gentle and lowly in heart, and you will find rest for your souls For My yoke is easy and My burden is light" (Matthew 11:29-30).

You are probably wondering why I have gone into such detail about the struggle in our marriage. I felt compelled of the Holy Spirit to share this with you because we live in an age where people give up too soon or lack the knowledge of God's Word to make it work. ***Hosea 4:6*** says, ***"My people are destroyed for a lack of knowledge..."*** We had no understanding of the principles found in the Bible concerning a husband and wife relationship, and I certainly grew up with no role models of wonderful marriages. The Bible asks us in **Amos 3:3** — ***"Can two walk together, unless they are agreed?"*** We have to agree with what God says. We have to know what He says concerning marriage because it is a picture of the love relationship between Jesus and the Church, which is us.

We began to put ***Ephesians 5:21-28*** into practice and lo and behold, God began to heal our marriage.

Submitting to one another in the fear of God. Wives, submit to your own husbands, as to the Lord. For the husband is head of the wife, as also Christ is head of the church; and He is the Savior of the body. Therefore, just as the church is subject to Christ, so let the wives be to their own husbands in everything. Husbands, love your wives, just as Christ also loved the church and gave Himself for her, that He might sanctify and cleanse her with the washing of water by the word, that He might present her to Himself a glorious church, not having spot or wrinkle or any such thing, but that she should be holy and without blemish.

So husbands ought to love their own wives as their own bodies; he who loves his wife loves himself.

A couple has to keep on working at their marriage. That means loving and forgiving whether one feels like it or not. We have to allow God's Word to have ascendancy in our lives rather than be led by our emotions or feelings because they change constantly; whereas, God never changes. We can depend on Him. Many people have a problem with the word "submit" because it has been abused. When used in the context of what God is saying through the Apostle Paul, it simply means a wife fits into her husband's plans gladly. He is not going to be a jerk and mistreat her, but he will give sacrificially of himself to her by loving and protecting her. Marriage is the death of two souls and two single wills being raised up as one entity.

Fulfill my joy by being like-minded, having the same love, being of one accord, of one mind. Let nothing be done through selfish ambition or conceit, but in lowliness of mind let each esteem others better than himself. Let each of you look out not only for his own interests, but also for the interests of others (Philippians 2:2-4).

It does not mean we lose our individual identity. It means we submit to one another in the fear of God. Where I am strong, Fred flows with me and vice versa. We have to trust God in each other, by being obedient to His Word. The Bibles says in ***Proverbs 3:5-6 — "Trust in the Lord with all your heart, And lean not on your own***

understanding; In all your ways acknowledge Him, And He shall direct your paths."

If we had not practiced the Word of God and fallen in love with Him, there would be no testimony. The key is to fall in love with Jesus first. We all come into a marriage with baggage from our past. We all come from some type of dysfunction. No family is perfect. Without the Perfect One, we cannot be complete. I wanted you to see how God worked in our lives in this area. He is always on the lookout for people who have a loyal heart towards Him. These are the kinds of people He can use to build His Kingdom on this earth. It simply means establishing His rule and reign on the earth, doing things His way, the righteous way.

For the eyes of the Lord run to and fro throughout the whole earth, to show Himself strong on behalf of those whose heart is loyal to Him (2 Chronicles 16:9).

This power and authority we have is based on our relationship with God. He empowers us to do great things on His behalf.

...The people who know their God shall be strong, and carry out great exploits (Daniel 11:32).

4

Our Heritage

Behold, children are a heritage from the Lord, The fruit of the womb is a reward.
Psalm 127:3

God has a sense of humor because as soon as we reconciled, I got pregnant with our son. He was born January 8, 1974. What a blessing! We named him Christopher Lee, but we call him Chris. His name means "Christ-Bearer" or "Follower of Christ." We did not know the meaning of his name at the time. This was prophetic because the Lord used him to draw us closer to each other and to cause us to follow Christ.

We dedicated him to the Lord while attending church with the family. Fred and I both loved to sing, so we joined the choir along with his mom who was the pianist, and his dad who was a tenor. I learned many hymns and the words were so comforting. It was another time for fellowship. We had begun attending Sunday school, and I also became involved in the women's ministry. This is where I learned about the Bible. I knew practically nothing, since my only religious knowledge had come from catechism. It was so refreshing hearing the Bible stories and principles of how to live. They were new to me. Fred was very knowledgeable of the Bible and I was impressed by it. I could ask him anything about the Bible, and he knew all the answers. We were feeling very happy and fulfilled. The void in our lives were being filled. It was due to the fact that we were experiencing the love of God through family and friends, which is what we desperately needed in our lives.

I remember reading the new church directory and saw Fred's and Chris' names and not mine. It really bothered me that I was excluded. I was not a member of the United Methodist Church we were attending, so I joined. I had to renounce Catholicism and that felt really strange at first. I wanted to be a part of my husband's and child's faith. The Bible was a little different, fewer books than the Jerusalem Bible, which the Catholics use.

After a year and a half, a new Pastor was sent to this church. There were rumors that he was Spirit-Filled. I did not have a clue what that meant. He was different. He prayed extemporaneously and unashamedly. He raised his hands when he prayed or worshiped God. He was happy and in love with Jesus. We had never seen this. We were intrigued and being drawn to God through this man. One Sunday in 1975, this Pastor invited people to come to the altar and be born again. I ran down from the choir loft to the chancel rail and knelt down, and felt my heart strangely warmed. I prayed a prayer of repentance and accepted Jesus as my Savior. I made a paradigm shift in my life. I took on Jesus as the center of my life and renounced my self-centeredness. I was born again!

Jesus answered and said to him, "Most assuredly, I say to you, unless one is born again, he cannot see the kingdom of God" (John 3:3).

I was encouraged to read the Bible, so that I could get to know God and take on His ways. ***Matthew 6:33*** became my motto for life—***But seek first the kingdom of God and His righteousness, and all these things shall be added to you.*** If I sought Him and lived for Him, He would take care of everything else and that has been proven over and over in my life. It truly was a new way of thinking and looking at things, and it could only happen by renewing my mind with God's Word. I realized that my thinking had to change in order for my attitude and behavior to change. ***Romans 12:2*** says, ***"And do not be conformed to this world, but be transformed by the renewing of your mind,..."*** This was the seventh year of our marriage, and the number seven in the Bible always means completion or perfection.

Chris was still a baby, and we were learning this new walk and how to apply the Christian principles. We were also learning how to be parents. He was our guinea pig. We believed what the Bible said about rearing children.

Train up a child in the way he should go, and when he is old, he will not depart from it (Proverbs 22:6).

All your children shall be taught of the Lord, And great shall be the peace of your children (Isaiah 54:13).

Not long after our conversion, our church had a Lay-Witness Mission. People from other churches came in and shared what Jesus had done in their lives, and how He had changed them and healed them physically and emotionally. This is where we met Cheryl Prewitt, now Salem, who later became Miss America in 1980. She was unashamedly, so full of boldness for the Lord. We had never seen that before. She told us she had power and was filled with the Holy Spirit and spoke in other tongues.

"But you shall receive power when the Holy Spirit has come upon you; and you shall be witnesses to Me in Jerusalem, and in all Judea and Samaria, and to the end of the earth" (Acts 1:8).

And they were all filled with the Holy Spirit and began to speak with other tongues, as the Spirit gave them utterance (Acts 2:4).

...They were all filled with the Holy Spirit, and they spoke the word of God with boldness (Acts 4:31).

She also told us how God had healed her and lengthened her leg after being in a terrible car wreck. She loved Jesus so much and was filled with His joy. We wanted what she had. She was a happy Christian and was positive. She had peace of mind and trusted in the Lord completely. So we prayed and gave our marriage and everything that we had to the Lord. Not long after that, we started a prayer group in our church. We were so hungry for more of God that we would gather with like-minded people and just pray. Nine months later in 1976, we were baptized in the Holy Spirit, and we spoke in tongues. Why tongues? It is the smallest member of our body and yet it can defile us. God wants control of our tongues. This is one of the evidences of being baptized in the Holy Spirit. God wants control of our tongues so He can keep us holy. This is what ***James 3:5-7*** speaks of:

"Even so the tongue is a little member and boasts great things. See how great a forest a little fire kindles! And the tongue is a fire, a world of iniquity. The tongue is so set among our members that it defiles the whole body, and sets on fire the course of nature; and it is set on fire by hell."

Tongues are a wonderful tool for praying. The Apostle Paul explains praying in tongues this way:

"For if I pray in a tongue, my spirit prays, but my understanding is unfruitful. What is the conclusion then? I will pray with the spirit, and I will also pray with the understanding. I will sing with the spirit, and I will also sing with the understanding" (1 Corinthians 14:14-15)

Jude 1:20-21 tells us tongues are used to encourage ourselves. ***"But you, beloved, building yourselves up on your most holy faith, praying in the Holy Spirit, keep yourselves in the love of God,..."***

That is when we were really converted. ***Psalm 40:1-3*** expresses what we felt:

"I waited patiently for the Lord; And He inclined to me, And heard my cry. He also brought me up out of a horrible pit, Out of the miry clay, And set my feet upon a rock, And established my steps. He has put a new song in my mouth—Praise to our God;..."

We saw Fred's family, and many other people experience what we had. Revival broke out in our church. People were changed. It was awesome! We had the joy of the Lord. We were bold and had His peace. Heaviness lifted. Worry lifted. Our trust in God was established. He was on the throne of our hearts. He would lead and direct us every step of the way, just as the Scripture says in ***Psalm 119:105 — "Your word is a lamp to my feet, And a light to my path."*** We had truly found a new way of living. This was in 1976, and we have never deviated from this experience. We were sealed with the Holy Spirit of God.

We began to truly serve in our local church. We were so grateful to God for what He had done in our lives that we wanted to serve Him with all of our hearts. Fred began to teach the men's Bible class, and then he became the Lay Leader, which is like being the Pastor's right hand. I taught the teenagers and got involved in the women's ministry. Our gifts made a place for us, and this is Scriptural. ***A man's gift makes room for him, And brings him before great men (Proverbs 18:16).*** Many would compliment Fred on his wonderful messages, his sermons. God was preparing him for the next phase of his life. We were growing in Christ because we were studying the Bible in order to teach, and it changed us. It changed our minds and hearts, so that our attitudes, our actions, and our behavior changed.

And do not be conformed to this world, but be transformed by the renewing of your mind, that you may prove what is that good and acceptable and perfect will of God (Romans 12:2).

It was a joy. We were happy and fulfilled. We did not know where all this was leading.

I began to want anther baby. In fact, I found ***Psalm 37:4*** that said, ***"Delight yourself also in the Lord, And He shall give you the desires of your heart."*** So I began to pray and declare this Scripture. I really felt in my heart that God was going to grant me this desire to show His faithfulness to His Word. I kept saying, "God is going to give me a blue-eyed, blond-haired daughter." Lo and behold, it happened! I was elated. We called her Denise, named after my baby sister. Her name means "wise discerner." Her first name is Valerie, at her dad's wish. She was a delightful baby. While carrying her, I took piano and voice lessons. I sang or played praise music all the time. This is what she listened to while in my womb. To this day, she is a worshipper. I believe she already had the joy of the Lord before she was born. In my opinion, it is as though she was filled with the Spirit in my womb like John the Baptist was in Elizabeth's womb. He leapt in her womb when Mary came to see her and it was because of Jesus being in her womb. Denise has always loved the Lord and used to play church as a little girl. Loving Jesus has been her whole life. When she was two years old, we were at a prayer meeting, and I heard this little voice praying in tongues. I opened my eyes and saw Denise's little hands raised, her eyes closed, and she was praying in the Spirit. It was so precious.

When Chris turned four, he wanted me to pray with him, so that he would know without a doubt that he had asked Jesus into his heart. He wanted to be sure he was a Christian. God gave me a Scripture for him, which is found in ***Luke 2:23 — ..." Every male who opens the womb shall be called holy to the Lord."*** This Scripture comes out of ***Exodus 13:2 — "Consecrate to Me all the firstborn, whatever opens the womb among the children of Israel, both of man and beast; it is Mine."***

I often reminded Chris that words carry weight. It was a declaration that He belonged to God because he was my firstborn. He was special, and the Lord was going to do great and mighty things through him.

Our children were a blessing to us and they still are. Chris was always very mischievous, and Denise was the perfect child. They attended public schools and being a teacher, I had the same schedule as they did. They were never latchkey kids or left unattended. We reared them on the Word of God. The Bible was our manual. We were not perfect parents but we had the Perfect One from Whom to learn. God had to have ascendancy in our lives. We were putting His principles to work.

Children, obey your parents in the Lord, for this is

right. "Honor your father and mother," which is the first commandment with promise: "that it may be well with you and you may live long on the earth" (Ephesians 6:1-3).

Not going to church was never an option. The kids knew they were going. They started out in the nursery when they were babies, then on to Children's Church until they were teenagers where they became part of the Youth Ministry. They went on fun trips and mission trips. Their social lives revolved mostly around the church. It does not mean they did not participate in school activities, it just means the bulk of their lives was spent with their church friends.

I believe as parents, it is our responsibility to be the parents, not their friends. We have to set boundaries for their own safety. We can become friends once they are adults. We have to realize that they are more than a physical body with an intellect, a will, and emotions. The Bible says in ***1 Thessalonians 5:23,*** we are a three part being.

Now may the God of peace Himself sanctify you completely; and may your whole spirit, soul, and body be preserved blameless at the coming of our Lord Jesus Christ.

That means we rear them according to the spirit (heart), the soul (intellect, will, emotions), and the physical body. Too many parents put all of the emphasis on the soul and the body and neglect the spirit. We insisted that they bathe and brush their teeth, eat the right things, study and read their school subjects, go to bed at a reasonable time to be fresh for school the next day, have regular dental and doctor checkups, etc. So why not go to church, read the Bible, learn to pray and get to know God, so that they can trust Him and be led by His Spirit? The spirit part has to be as real and natural to them as the soul and the body.

After graduation from high school, both Chris and Denise chose to go to Christ For The Nations Bible Institute in Dallas, Texas. They chose this route of their own volition. We always allowed them to make their own decisions and work out their own relational problems and issues. The Word of God directed their lives. They were not perfect, but they were in process. They were good PK's (preacher's kids)!

In fact, Chris went through a season where he said he would never teach or preach because he said all we ever did was read, write, and stand before people and teach or preach. He wanted no part of that. God does have a sense of humor because this is what he does best.

Denise went through her own crisis where she felt totally "boxed in" because her mother taught at her school, her father was the Pastor at church, her uncle Rick was the Youth Pastor at that time, and her brother was part of the same youth ministry. In spite of this, they both became role models for young people.

Let no one despise your youth, but be an example to

the believers in word, in conduct, in love, in spirit, in faith, in purity (1 Timothy 4:12).

After Bible school, Chris came back to Memphis and worked for a couple of years in our academy and with the youth ministry as an intern. He also attended our Bible school while performing these duties. Then he went on the road for a year as a team leader for a traveling drama ministry called "Forecast." While on the road, he married a Canadian girl, Becky Mediwake, in 1997. He met her two years prior when he went up to Alberta to a Youth Conference. It truly is a testimony of God's plan and purpose by putting two people together in order to accomplish His will. He and Becky settled in Minneapolis to help pastor and pioneered a church. He returned to us after four and a half years to become an Associate Pastor, establishing our Care Pastor Ministry, reorganizing the Men's Ministry and becoming his dad's right hand. He is also a great preacher with revelation beyond his years. He came home with his wife and our first grandbaby, Maia, in December of 2000. By the time this book is printed, there will be a second grandbaby, a boy this time. We stood on ***Isaiah 60:4 — Your sons shall come from afar, And your daughters shall be nursed by your side.***

...That your children shall come back to their own border (Jeremiah 31:17).

We believe God spoke to us through His Word. We are delighted they are with us. However, this came as a result of us delighting ourselves in the Lord. It was the desire of our hearts (Psalm 37:4).

Denise went on the road immediately after Bible school with the same drama group and then returned home to be a youth intern. She then became the Associate Youth Pastor. She is very gifted and anointed in relating to teenagers. She is such a blessing. She also sings from time to time on the praise team. God often gives her prophetic songs that just melt me. She is a great and anointed preacher, too.

They have both traveled extensively in the world. They truly have a kingdom worldview. They have ministered in the U.S., Canada, Europe, the Philippines, and on the Reservations to the Native Americans. Chris has been to Australia and New Zealand and Denise to India and Turkey. They will carry on with the vision because they are very bold, they are very prophetic, and they have a no-nonsense attitude and a low tolerance for religious spirits and sin. Most of all, they are called of God, chosen before the foundation of the world for this work. They have destiny written all over them.

"...Those who are with Him are called, chosen, and faithful" (Revelation 17:14).

Our Wedding Day

July 23, 1968 - Fred & Val

Answering the Call

The Bennetts 1978
Fred, Val, Chris (4½) & Denise (1½)

A Service at Piperton UMC - 1978

Our Family - Fred's parents and two grandmothers

Pioneering Christ The Rock 1983

Family Portrait 1995

Becky & Chris' Wedding - January 3, 1997

Family Picture with First Grandchild, Maia
2002

5
The Call

Who has saved us and called us with a holy calling, not according to our works, but according to His own purpose and grace...
2 Timothy 1:9

Not long after the birth of our daughter, Fred told me that he felt God calling him to go into the ministry. I told him, "No way!" I was not going to be a minister's wife. In fact, I told him that he needed to forget about it. I had not married a preacher, and I was not going to be married to one either. I was perfectly happy being a homemaker loving and serving God. I had taught school for five years prior, and knew that one day I would resume my teaching career once my children went to school. I just could not fathom the idea of being in the ministry. Besides that, a pastor's wife was called "Sister," and all I could see were nuns wearing habits. That was a "turnoff" for me. I even went to our pastor and told him that Fred would probably be coming in to tell him that he feels called to the ministry. My advice to him was that he was to tell Fred that it was not so. I was using manipulation because I was fearful. Fred never broached the subject again and that was so out of character for him. He had to trust God where I was concerned.

It was so strange knowing this in my heart of hearts and yet I could not accept this call—this unknown lifestyle. I was in denial. I struggled with the call because I did not know if I could drink the cup I felt I was being presented. I did not want to go against God's will for our lives. I knew that the only safe place was "smack dab" in the center of His will. I knew God enough by now to realize that this was His best for us. I did not want a life without Him. Been there, done that! I was so timid and such an introvert at that time. Being in the ministry is such a public expression and lifestyle. I did not know if I was cut out for this awesome call. I sought God even more and came to the realization that I had to die to myself. I had to die to feelings of fear, inferiority and being introverted. The thought crossed my mind, "What will my family think?" I already felt like they thought I was in a cult because I had left the Catholic faith. I had to die to what people thought about me. I was always such a people pleaser because of insecurities.

...,"If anyone desires to come after Me, let him deny himself, and take up his cross, and follow Me. For whoever desires to save his life will lose it, but whoever loses his life for My sake will find it" (Matthew 16:24-25).

I was new at this walk of faith, only two years old, and God had not finished changing and freeing me from all the excess baggage that I had been carrying around for so long. I had to bury the past and press on to the upward call of God on our lives. The Apostle Paul says it very well in ***Philippians 3:14 — "I press toward the goal for the prize of the upward call of God in Christ Jesus."***

One year later, I truly felt the call and was ready to accept it no matter the cost. I knew without a shadow of a doubt that we were called together, so I told Fred. He had been waiting for me to realize this. I am not one who jumps into things easily. I am too pragmatic which is sometimes detrimental. We went to our pastor and let him know we were ready for the ministry, so he informed the District Superintendent. Fred spoke with him and asked to be assigned to any little church that could not afford a part time pastor. We just wanted to serve. We were told this was never done in the denomination and yet we felt like this is what God wanted us to do. In my heart I thought, "We will see." ...***And it is the Spirit who bears witness, because the Spirit is truth (1 John 5:6).***

Two weeks later, the District Superintendent called Fred and told him there was an opening for a part time pastor. Praise God! We knew this was God. We were sent to Piperton United Methodist Church, in the Memphis District, in June 1978. We had been Christians for three years. God did a quick work.

Fred had to go back to the university to get his Business Administration Degree, which he obtained in December 1979. He went on to seminary on the G.I. Bill (veterans' benefits) for his Master of Divinity Degree. This was a requirement of the denomination. When he began seminary, I also went back to the university so that

I could return to teaching. My heart was to get back to my career and teach high school French. Thank God for the military and thank God for Pell Grants. The U.S. Government paid for our education. What a blessing! We were in school from January 1980 until May 1983. I would never recommend both husband and wife going to school at the same time, in addition to being parents, but we did it by the grace of God. We arranged it so that one of us was home with the children. We both finished our education at the end of our five-year tenure at Piperton United Methodist Church. We felt we had accomplished what God called us to do there. It was a great place to learn all the phases of the ministry. Most of all, we learned about faith, believing God to supply our every need, from food and clothing, to money to pay the bills. Why? Salaries were minimal and I believed it was also a test to see if we were truly called.

That the genuineness of your faith, being much more precious than gold that perishes, though it is tested by fire, may be found to praise, honor, and glory at the revelation of Jesus Christ (1 Peter 1:7).

God does not tempt us, but He does test us. Temptations are for our destruction whereas tests are for our growth. Temptation is a tool of the devil to cause us to fail.

God provided for everything. It was amazing. There were days when I had to pray for food to come so that I could feed my family. Sure enough, it would manifest. Someone would knock on the door and say that God told them to bless us. We never told people what we needed.

We told God. We learned early on that if you tell people, they will help and sometimes they feel manipulated or obligated into doing so. We told God and He came through every time. This is just one example. I could write a book only on His provision. His Word really works.

And my God shall supply all your need according to His riches in glory by Christ Jesus (Philippians 4:19).

While there, we grew from thirty-five to three hundred. Wow! We needed more space, so we got into our first building program. We renovated the sanctuary and added a Fellowship Hall. Most of the people that joined were not Methodists. They were from various denominations such as Baptist, Presbyterian, Catholic, but mostly Pentecostal and Charismatic. They were not attached to their denomination. We taught on the Holy Spirit and the principles of the Bible and the people came. They were hungry for truth and freedom. ***John 8:32*** says, "***And you shall know the truth, and the truth shall make you free.***" We were amazed that they would come because in our own eyes we felt so unworthy. We demonstrated Jesus' love and that drew them. Jesus said in **John 12:32** – "***And I, if I am lifted up from the earth, will draw all peoples to Myself.***" This was a sign of how we were beginning to embrace all kinds of people. It began with the various religious groups. We were not boxed into the denomination.

During those five years there, I believe we were pregnant with the vision of Christ The Rock Metro Church.

We knew there was something beyond Piperton United Methodist Church, and God would show us when the time was right because He started us on this exciting journey of faith.

...He who has begun a good work in you will complete it until the day of Jesus Christ (Philippians 1:6).

There was an excitement in our bosom. We had felt it in our last and fifth year there. We were going to have to give up Fred's salary, his retirement, and his medical insurance and live by faith. We were going to start over and we had the grace for it.

Now faith is the substance of things hoped for, the evidence of things not seen (Hebrews 11:1).

The call was getting clearer and nearer. He used Piperton UMC to test the call and our faithfulness to Him. **Revelation 17:14** tells us "*...**For He is Lord of lords and King of kings; and those who are with Him are called, chosen and faithful.***" The true purpose was to pioneer Christ The Rock Metro Church because God wanted a different kind of church for Memphis. We would live to see it unfold.

For the vision is yet for an appointed time; But at the end it will speak, and it will not lie. Though it tarries, wait for it; Because it will surely come, It will not tarry (Habakkuk 2:3).

6

Pioneering

Unless the Lord builds the house,
They labor in vain who build it;...
Psalm 127:1

As mentioned in chapter one, we had gone on a long needed vacation after having graduated from the university and seminary. Upon our return, we gathered with a few people in our living room and shared with them that it was time for the vision to come forth. It was time to birth a different kind of charismatic independent church. This meeting took place in July 1983. The next step was to inform the District Superintendent of the denomination. We did, and he gave us two weeks notice. Now there definitely was no turning back! It was either make it or break it! Fred formed a board of men who had this same vision. There was unity and agreement and excitement.

Behold, how good and how pleasant it is For brethren to dwell together in unity! ...For there the Lord commanded the blessing—Life forevermore (Psalm 133:1 & 3).

We had looked at buildings and nothing felt right. Nothing bore witness with our spirits. The day after we returned from vacation, we found a five-acre parcel of land between Collierville and Germantown on Houston Levee Road. It was a perfect location for a church. We knew we had to build because God had spoken this Scripture to us — ***"And let them make Me a sanctuary, that I may dwell among them" (Exodus 25:8).*** We needed $3000 as earnest money for a down payment. All we had in our newly formed account was $33. We were in faith for the balance. ***For who has despised the day of small things? ...(Zechariah 4:10).***

We had one more Sunday in the denomination before departing. We believed in fulfilling our commitment. Fred's last sermon came out of Genesis where Abraham and Lot's men were quarreling over land. He saw that this was unnecessary and that there was plenty of good land for every one.

So Abram said to Lot, "Please let there be no strife between you and me,..." (Genesis 13:8).

...And they separated from each other (Genesis 13:11).

Abraham decided to leave in peace and we did the same thing. The separation was amicable and painful. There was a feeling of closure and relief. We knew our time and purpose there was over. We had fulfilled God's plan there. The church of thirty-five people had grown to three hundred. The original members of the church wanted their building back and God had other plans for us. Our vision was different from theirs. We wanted to move with God, and they wanted the status quo. To each his own! It was time for us to leave in peace.

Pursue peace with all people, and holiness, without which no one will see the Lord (Hebrews 12:14).

In the mean time, Fred had to find a facility for this new congregation. The first door opened to us was the VFW (Veterans of Foreign Wars) Club. The first Sunday, of August 1983, Christ The Rock Church was born. One hundred twenty-five people showed up, including children. We never expected that many people. God surprised us to say the least. We outgrew this place for a Sunday morning service, so we began to meet at the old Germantown Community Center and continued at the VFW club on Wednesday evenings. This was the month that I resumed my career as a French teacher at Bartlett High School after having been a homemaker and a part time student for ten years.

We had a month to raise the money for the down payment on the land. Glory to God, we got it almost to the dollar. We also had a charter membership Sunday, and we ended up with one hundred forty-five people. So, we broke ground and built an all purpose facility. It really was a gym with offices, a nursery, and classrooms. We were in it within a year and a half of having begun this church—January 1985. What a miracle! What a quick work! The reason we were able to buy and build so quickly was that our overhead on Sundays and Wednesdays was minimal. How many charismatic independent churches own land and build a church and are in it in within a year and a half? God is good. His hand has always been on us. The Scripture says in ***Psalm 139:10 — Even there Your hand shall lead me, And Your right hand shall hold me.*** This is our genesis, where this mighty work started.

God began to grow us again right after we moved into our new facility at 3505 Houston Levee Road. God directed us by His Word to build again.

Enlarge the place of your tent, And let them stretch out the curtains of your dwellings; Do not spare; Lengthen your cords, And strengthen your stakes. For you shall expand to the right and to the left, And your descendants will inherit the nations, And make the desolate cities inhabited (Isaiah 54:2-3).

In the mean time, we leased a doublewide trailer to help facilitate the needed classroom space until the annex was completed in 1991. It housed a chapel, a fellowship hall and more classrooms. Praise God! At first our growth was based on people coming from other denominations that wanted to experience praise and worship. We did not use hymnals, but contemporary choruses based on Scripture that we projected on an overhead screen. We have always been a cutting edge church in the area of music. We have always had great sermons that were relative to every day living. We were a different kind of church. We have never had phenomenal growth spurts. It has always been steady and on going. We saw the denominational walls of division come down, so we began to pray for the racial barrier to be destroyed. We sought God for "all kinds of people". We wanted to see the Kingdom of God manifest in our midst. We wanted to see a picture of heaven on earth, a place where there was unity.

We had always felt that Memphis needed a training center to raise up godly five fold ministries, a place to train the saints and psalmists that would lead us into God's presence through praise and worship.

And He Himself gave some to be apostles, some prophets, some evangelists, and some pastors and teachers, for the equipping of the saints for the work of ministry, for the edifying of the body of Christ,... (Ephesians 4:11-12).

There were no Bible schools in Memphis that we knew of. The Lord sent us Dr. Stephen Nielsen, an anointed brother in the Lord, who founded our Memphis Bible Institute and Christ The Rock Christian Academy in August 1993. It truly was in God's heart. The key Scripture for our schools is found in ***Proverbs 4:7 — Wisdom is the principal thing; Therefore get wisdom. And in all your getting, get understanding.*** Fred and I attended our Bible school and earned Doctorate Degrees of Theology.

We continued to grow and we needed more space. We had filled this building. We were up to seven hundred members. The word out of ***Isaiah 54:2-3*** was given to us again. ***Enlarge the place of your tent, And let them stretch out the curtains of your dwellings; Do not spare; Lengthen your cords, And strengthen your stakes. For you shall expand to the right and to the left, And your descendants will inherit the nations, And***

make the desolate cities inhabited. It always came from different guest speakers who were moving under the anointing of the Spirit. God was always confirming His Word, always directing.

We remained at our Houston Levee address for a total of eleven years. We purchased twenty acres on Winchester Road in Memphis in 1994. It is about two miles from the first location. We did not know that this part of Memphis would eventually be called the Technology Corridor that includes the World Headquarters of Federal Express, Nike, and other enterprises. A new thoroughfare, the Nonconnah Parkway, was built to connect this part of the city with the rest of Memphis. What a Godsend! It is just down the road from our new location! We were moving into the city, and it seemed like everyone was moving out to the suburbs.

In July of 1995, we broke ground. We were getting ready to build phase one of a brand new facility at this new location. For Fred and I, it was building number four. We were getting used to this way of life by now. God said enlarge, so we obeyed. That was all there was to it! During that time we had been hosting a half-hour television program, "A Drink From The Rock", every Sunday morning on a local secular channel that ran for five years. We did not renew the contract due to our building program. In fact, in 1984, we had had a fifteen-minute program by the same name, which ran six years, Monday through Friday on a local Christian radio station. We were cancelled when new owners took over, because they objected to women preachers, namely me.

We sold our facility at Houston Levee Road and were able to lease it back for a year. Praise God! It took more than a year and a half to complete our new facility, so we had to move to temporary quarters until our facility was finished. This is not a problem when one is small but when in excess of seven hundred, it is difficult to find an appropriate location with enough space to accommodate everyone. We ended up leasing the Home Builders Association located on Germantown Parkway in Cordova from April until November 1996. We could only meet there on Sundays for our services, so we leased office space in Collierville. It was an uncomfortable time not having a place to call our own. We felt as though we were in the wilderness. This is where the cloud directed us. We agreed that being nomads was for the birds! We did grow while in Cordova. We were exposed to people that had never heard about us, so our sphere of influence was growing. We were becoming more and more of a city church. Every time we drove by the construction site, we would shout this Scripture ***Zechariah 4:7 — ...With shouts of "Grace, grace to it!"*** To us it felt like we were speeding up the process.

Finally, we were in our new sanctuary on the first Sunday of November 1996. The rest of the building was completed by the end of December that same year. We were back to one service, all worshipping together again as one family. We were so excited to be in this new building. We thought we could rest from construction for the next ten years. We could chill out! We rejoiced and could not thank God enough for what He had accomplished through His people.

Praise the Lord! Sing to the Lord a new song, And His praise in the assembly of saints (Psalm 149:1).

We knew it was all God and He had done it by His Spirit with an obedient people. ***Zechariah 4:6*** says, ***"...Not by might nor by power, but by My Spirit, Says the Lord of hosts."***

We added "Metro" to the name since we were gradually becoming a city church. From that time on we were **Christ The Rock Metro Church**. It was so wonderful to be worshiping in a real sanctuary, not a gymnasium like we had from 1985 until 1996. We had padded chairs instead of plastic ones. We did not have stripes on the floor, a Coca Cola scoreboard on the wall, or basketball goals. It was pretty and it had ambiance. We grew again. It is God who gives the increase (1 Corinthians 3:7).

Right after our grand opening in 1997, it became a year of transition for us. It was a year of great joys, trials, and tribulations. Once again we had to die to what we knew and what was comfortable. Certain events in our lives hastened the process.

"These things I have spoken to you, that in Me you may have peace. In the world you will have tribulation; but be of good cheer, I have overcome the world" (John 16:33).

On January 3, 1997, Chris and Becky married in Alberta, Canada. It was the most wonderful and precious wedding we had ever experienced. They also informed us that the ministry they were serving would be moving to

Minneapolis, so that meant they were going too. This broke our hearts because we wanted them with us in the ministry.

Then on the 14th of this same month, Fred's mother passed away. She had been fighting Leukemia for quite some time. It broke our hearts because we loved her so much. She was the glue that held the family together. She was such a giver and an exhorter. She was a wonderful mother and "mamaw." It was a very difficult time for us as a family. God was comforting us. His Spirit, also called the Helper, was ministering to us (John 14:26). He gave us peace in knowing that we will one day see her when we get to Heaven.

And the peace of God, which surpasses all understanding, will guard your hearts and minds through Christ Jesus (Philippians 4:7).

Denise went on the road with the traveling drama ministry of which Chris had been a part after graduating from Christ For The Nations Institute in May. We were prepared because this is something she had anticipated doing. Upon arriving at school, she tried out and made the drama team. She had always been very gifted in acting when she was in the youth ministry of the church. Even knowing her plans, it was difficult to let "our baby" go. We really did not know what she was going to do after her commitment with them. We did not know whether or not she would be coming back home either.

The Lord was also leading me to give up my teaching career and become Women's Pastor at the church. I loved my job, I loved the teachers with whom I worked, and I loved the students. This season of my life was coming to an end. It was a time of inner turmoil for me. I knew God wanted me to lay it down and I had a hard time letting go. I had a wrestling match with God. It was a battle of wills—my will or His.

Father, if it is Your will, take this cup away from Me; nevertheless not My will, but Yours, be done (Luke 22:42).

Besides being a mother and a wife, being a teacher was the only other identity I had known. I had come to the place in my life where I was used to having my salary and being able to make purchases whenever I so desired. I had become independent in a sense. Early on, when we were pioneering the church, I did not want to feel obligated to the congregation. I did not know the Word of God. ***"...The laborer is worthy of his wages" (1 Timothy 5:18).*** It is a righteous act for the body to support the ministry. I had a poverty mentality and needed teaching of God's Word concerning owning material things. I realized that it was okay for Christians to have nice things as long as these things did not possess them and that they realize that God was the source of their blessings.

And you shall remember the Lord your God, for it is He who gives you power to get wealth, that He may establish His covenant which He swore to your fathers, as it is this day (Deuteronomy 8:18).

I was accustomed to my earnings and now I was going to have to depend solely on the Lord to meet my needs. I was counting the cost.

For which of you, intending to build a tower, does not sit down first and count the cost, whether he has enough to finish it (Luke 14:28).

Could I truly trust Him that much? The answer was yes. He is true to His Word. ***Then the Lord said to me, "You have seen well, for I am ready to perform My word" (Jeremiah 1:12).*** I submitted to His will for my life. Besides that, I would rather be in God's will than anywhere else. That is where I experience perfect peace. So I wrote my letter of resignation in April and informed the congregation. These dear souls gave me a standing ovation. God was leading me and they had seen God moving in my life, and they were in agreement with what He was doing. ***The steps of a good man are ordered by the Lord, And He delights in his way (Psalm 37:23).*** We have to be open to change in our lives. God is always bringing forth His plans and purposes in our lives. He knows best and we have to trust Him.

For I know the thoughts that I think toward you, says the Lord, thoughts of peace and not of evil, to give you a future and a hope (Jeremiah 29:11).

Not teaching, was an adjustment for me at first. I had to realize that my true identity was in Jesus and not in being "Madame Bennett," the French teacher. God had been unfolding His plans for me and I had to be obedient. It was a new day with new challenges. He told me I would be an "ear" for a season and not a "mouth." In other words, He was going to teach me how to listen and counsel and then He would open a new door for me to teach. I would be teaching the Bible this time rather than French. This other door has opened to me to preach and teach in French, in the Francophone world. What a blessing! That is even more exciting. He has met all of my needs in unique ways.

...But one thing I do, forgetting those things which are behind and reaching forward to those things which are ahead, I press toward the goal for the prize of the upward call of God in Christ Jesus (Philippians 3:13-14).

So here we were, "empty nesters," and it was a difficult time, a time of feeling empty! Many parents are relieved to be rid of their children. We did not feel that way at all because we missed them so much. We always enjoyed them and wanted them with us in the ministry. They were always so much fun because of their unique personalities and sense of humor. In fact if we had our way, they could live with us, too. We had chosen long ago that we were going to serve Him in good times and difficult times.

..."But as for me and my house, we will serve the Lord" (Joshua 24:15).

In the midst of all this, Christ The Rock Metro Church was growing. We went to two services again. God has always been faithful to fill what we build. We also needed a gymnasium because of all the team sports and youth activities we had. Our people were tired of going from one place to another to practice and play. We needed another building program. We needed a gym. The construction of building number five began four years later and was completed in November of 2000. We built it with a dual purpose in mind. Later on it could be converted into a school with classrooms to accommodate our academy and also serve the Sunday school ministry. What an exciting time! It also gave us more space for wedding receptions and sit down meals for conferences and seminars. Our fellowship hall could no longer accommodate the numbers.

Holding two services caused us to grow and the Word of the Lord came again out of Isaiah 54 about enlarging our tent. We had to obey God. Now our faith was going to be stretched to the limits. The original vision was to have a large visible auditorium in order to raise up a great army that would put fear in the enemy's camp and bring about unity in the city of Memphis. After all, we are a people of faith and have chosen to live that way.

For in it the righteousness of God is revealed from faith to faith; as it is written, "The just shall live by faith" (Romans 1:17).

We embarked on a building campaign to raise the finances required to build phase three, our 3000 seat auditorium. This meant building number six for us. Building is not easy because it means going to the next level and there is so much spiritual warfare involved. It has been that way every time we have built and it does not get any easier. That is why we have to have on our spiritual armor, pray, and confess the Word of God over ourselves.

Finally, my brethren, be strong in the Lord and in the power of His might. Put on the whole armor of God, that you may be able to stand against the wiles of the devil. For we do not wrestle against flesh and blood, but against principalities, against powers, against the rulers of the darkness of this age, against spiritual hosts of wickedness in the heavenly places. Therefore take up the whole armor of God, that you may be able to withstand in the evil day, and having done all, to stand. Stand therefore, having girded your waist with truth, having put on the breastplate of righteousness, and having shod your feet with the preparation of the gospel of peace; above all, taking the shield of faith with which you will be able to quench all the fiery darts of the wicked one. And take the helmet of salvation, and the sword of the Spirit, which is the word of God; praying always with all prayer and supplication in the Spirit, being watchful to this end with all perseverance and supplication for all the saints—(Ephesians 6:10-18).

God spoke to us nineteen years ago about building this great work. It was not an ego trip. It was God's Word to us. This is a testimony of what He can do through a group of people who love Him. It would be a mighty church, a prototype, one of a kind, that would show forth the truth and be a standard of righteousness. The Word spoken over this body of believers is found in the Gospel of ***Matthew 5:14-16:***

You are the light of the world. A city that is set on a hill cannot be hidden. Nor do they light a lamp and put it under a basket, but on a lampstand, and it gives light to all who are in the house. Let your light so shine before men, that they may see your good works and glorify your Father in heaven.

In July 2001, we broke ground. What a blessing! The vision was finally happening. It has taken many steps to get there but that is the way God works. I was so honored that my dear mother was visiting me and took part in this celebration. It was such an exciting time because she got to see and experience first hand what God was doing in our midst. We, as a congregation, celebrated the Lord and how awesome He is. ***Lord, our Lord, How excellent is Your name in all the earth (Psalm 8:1).***

Construction began in September 2001. It would take a little over a year so that meant we would be living in a construction zone. It was better than going to other quarters. It has truly been amazing to watch the facility be built and to see the renovations made to the present building to accommodate the change. It is unbelievable. We are doubly blessed because God brought our children home to be with us and to share in this momentous time. Words cannot express what we feel. God is true to His Word. That which He promised long ago is coming to pass. We will be in the new sanctuary in October of 2002. We have no idea what all God is going to do. He has always been faithful in filling every facility, and He has also expanded the ministry to touch more people.

Eye has not seen, nor ear heard, Nor have entered into the heart of man The things which God has prepared for those who love Him (1 Corinthians 2:9).

...For they drank of that spiritual Rock that followed them, and that Rock was Christ (1 Corinthians 10:4).
It was out of this Scripture that we received the name of our church.

On the following pages are pictures from our beginning to where we are now.

First Pastorate

Piperton United Methodist Church
1978 - 1983

Piperton United Methodist Church
Fellowship Hall
1981

First Meeting Place

VFW (Veterans Foreign Wars) Club - Collierville
Wednesday Evenings 1983-1985

Germantown Community Center
Sundays 1983 - 1985

Christ The Rock Church

Houston Levee
1985 - 1996

Annex 1990

Homebuilders

Temporary Quarters
April 1996 - November 1996

Christ The Rock Metro Church - Phase I

8800 Winchester
November 1996

Phase II

Inside Gymnasium - 2000

Christ The Rock Christian Academy 2002

Ground -Breaking for New Sanctuary
July 2001

The building began September 2001
to be completed October 2002

7
A Prophetic Church

...For the testimony of Jesus is the spirit of prophecy.
Revelation 19:10

God has called Christ The Rock Metro Church to be a prophetic church. We are now a church of two thousand members. He has individually hand picked each one for a specific purpose.

But now God has set the members, each one of them, in the body just as He pleased (1 Corinthians 12:18).

As a church body, we have been called to be a sign and a wonder in this city and to this generation. We were told long ago that only homogenous churches grow and make a difference in their communities. We knew in our heart of hearts that we needed a manifestation of Heaven on earth. It had to start in the church, a safe place where all kinds of people could come together. We are still "walking it out" and have come to the conclusion that God meant for Christians to be leading the way rather than being at the tail end. They were to be a new breed of people with a new mindset. The old biases will have to die in order to establish this new order. God is defining a new culture.

According to Webster's Dictionary, **Culture** is defined as:

1. Fineness of feelings, thoughts, tastes, manners;
2. Civilization of a given race or nation at a given time;
3. Development of the mind or body by education, training;
4. Preparation of the land to raise crops by plowing, planting, and necessary care; cultivation;
5. Proper care given to raising of animals or plants;
6. Colony or growth of germs of a given kind that has been carefully made for a special purpose.

God is doing something brand new in the midst of us. He is refining us to treat others as ourselves by loving whomever He sends.

A new commandment I give to you, that you love one another; as I have loved you, that you also love one another. By this all will know that you are My disciples, if you have love for one another (John 13:34-35).

He is definitely establishing a new civilization among us by bringing the nations to our body. We have people from all corners of the earth. The Bible tells us in ***Psalm 2:8 — "Ask of Me, and I will give You The nations for Your inheritance, And the ends of the earth for Your possession."*** The Word of God has been educating and training us all these years to have open hearts for all kinds of people. It has not come automatically or naturally, it is a learned heart behavior. We have had to carefully prepare by plowing and planting, and then caring for the new growth. Ministry is work.

See, I have this day set you over the nations and over the kingdoms, To root out and to pull down, To destroy and to throw down, To build and to plant (Jeremiah 1:10).

We are a new colony in a growth medium with a specific purpose. Our church is truly a prototype of nations and races coming together. We are still in the process of walking this out but with God's direction and the anointing of the Holy Spirit, we shall.

We are prophetic in that we are givers. We give with God's Kingdom in mind, which includes His plans and purposes. We approach giving with an urgency to see the vision fulfilled. We believe in and teach tithing. It means giving God the first tenth of our income.

"Bring all the tithes into the storehouse, That there may be food in My house, And try Me now in this," Says the LORD of hosts, "If I will not open for you the windows of heaven And pour out for you such blessing That there will not be room enough to receive it" (Malachi 3:10).

We obey the Word of God by practicing its principles. When we first became Christians we did not know how we were going to tithe. Our bills looked overwhelming, but we knew we had to obey the Word. It takes faith to obey God's Word and it is a choice. We have never lacked since we have been giving tithes and offerings. In fact, God has blessed us tremendously and we attribute it to tithing and giving of alms to the poor and sowing as God directs.

As a prophetic church, we have our identity in Jesus Christ. After the new birth, we are new creations, and the old man is dead. The Holy Spirit has come to abide in us in order to change us. Our spirit is instantly changed, but our soul (intellect, will, emotions) is changed over a process of time. It is like moving into an old house, and Jesus, the Expert Carpenter, has to tear out the old and remodel it to make it brand new.

Therefore, if anyone is in Christ, he is a new creation; old things have passed away; behold, all things have become new (2 Corinthians 5:17).

We learn to walk by the Spirit by allowing Him to make the necessary changes in our lives, ridding us of old habits. We become what we focus on. Since we identify with the Lord, we focus on Him. Jesus, the Word made flesh is our mirror.

...He who practices righteousness is righteous, just as He is righteous (1 John 3:7) .

Being a prophetic church is a challenge to the status quo. We have to remain on the cutting edge to be effective in this world. It is time for the Church as a whole to be in the driver's seat leading the way. We must make a difference and leave a legacy to the next generation. We must communicate and impart these new cultural values such as: being a non-conformist towards the worldview, righteousness through faith, and the revelation of the ascendancy of the Word of God for practice in life. That is our hope and prayer through the founding of Christ The Rock Metro Church. It is a wonderful place to be rooted and grounded if your desire is to be a new race—a part of a new culture.

But you are a chosen generation, a royal priesthood, a holy nation, His own special people, that you may proclaim the praises of Him who called you out of darkness into His marvelous light; who once were not a people but are now the people of God, who had not obtained mercy but now have obtained mercy (1 Peter 2:9-10).

Phase III

To be continued...